JACK ROSE's
Changing
LOWESTOFT

with
Dean Parkin

Rushmere
Publishing

First published 1994 by Rushmere Publishing
32 Rushmere Road, Carlton Colville, Lowestoft, Suffolk

Second impression 1996

Typeset by Chemtech Graphics
Sussex Road, Gorleston, Norfolk

Printed in England by Blackwell John Buckle
Charles Street, Great Yarmouth, Norfolk, NR30 3LA

ISBN 1 872992 08 0

Printed on recycled paper

Acknowledgements

Such was the help and support of so many, that I could have dedicated this book to a long list of people and nearly did.

Hopefully a special word of thanks here will do the job. Top of the list are the photographers and their wives, that's Kenny and Ann Carsey, Rix and Hilary Turrell, and Colin and Jan Bryant who have always been ready to help me and are good friends too. Bert Collyer is another who went out of his way to help, providing prints and the photograph on the back cover, while I am grateful to Simon Baker for his contribution in taking the modern pictures.

Thanks are also given to Gordon Steward, Roy Capps, Ken Jarmin, H. Browne, Archie Durrant, 'Dickie' Bird, Peter Killby, Jessie Verrall, Sylvia Reeve, Margaret Barley, Rosemary Pye, June Burgess, Philip Croft, Joyce Moore and departed friends Ford Jenkins, Jack Mitchley and Wally Holden for their readiness over the years to supply me with photographs.

Dedicated to
Lowestoftians everywhere!

Disappeared

In 1973 it was announced that St. John's was to close but there were hopes that the church would remain standing and perhaps be used for another purpose, such as a museum. However, as early as 1964 St. John's soft stone had been crumbling badly and like so many buildings in the town, the 1953 floods had caused a great deal of damage with salt still coming through the walls up to its demolition.

By January 1978 St. John's Church was a ruin. Although the Lowestoft Archaeological and Local History Society had wanted to buy the church's famous clock, when they arrived on the site it was too late as it had already been sold to a Solihull enthusiast for just £150.

The demolition of St. John's Church in December 1977 began with the spire. Opened in July 1894 this church was erected in less than a year, although its famous clock wasn't added until 1897. During the war its spire was considered to be too much of a landmark and was camouflaged with canvas, which was soon blown away in the easterly winds. The army tied it on again, backing the canvas with wire netting, but that soon became detached and the attempt to camouflage one of Lowestoft's most famous landmarks was abandoned.

The Central Methodist Church on the corner of London Road North and Gordon Road, pictured here after the War with the spire removed due to its poor condition. The church was badly damaged during the wartime bombing and never re-opened. The empty building was chiefly appreciated by the thousands of pigeons that used it as a resting place and when it was finally pulled down in July 1956 the pigeons had an abrupt change of religion and transferred their allegiance to the Roman Catholic Church in Gordon Road. Never has a church received so many unwelcome converts!

The building of the *Royal Hotel* began in 1849 and the hotel opened a year later. Architecturally, it was declared one of the best commercial buildings in the country and by the time it was demolished in 1973, the hotel's façade had changed very little, despite narrowly missing a German bombardment in World War One and the blitz of World War Two. During the last war the hotel was requisitioned by the Admiralty in 1941 and for a full five years became known as H.M.S. Mantis. In 1946 it was derequisitioned and on June 8th 1947 re-opened as an hotel. The site of the hotel is now occupied by the new East Point Pavilion.

It is said that Charles Dickens once visited the *Royal* and so did King George V, although neither stayed the night.

Photographs showing the demolition of the *Suffolk Hotel* in the early 1970s. The hotel, built in 1873, was owned by the Yarmouth brewery of E. Lacon & Son who gave up the lease in 1966 though the hotel traded for a few more years before finally closing in 1971. In December 1971 the demolition of the *Suffolk Hotel* began and in August 1972 a £150,000 redevelopment of the site was announced to start in November and a new Lipton's shop was built.

On Monday 26th July, 1966, the former Palace cinema, having recently been converted into a bingo hall, was destroyed in a spectacular fire and here is shown its charred remains. The fire was first spotted when smoke began to pour from the building at around midnight. A glowing spot was then seen on the roof which suddenly burst into flames causing the asbestos sheeting to explode. Newspapers reported that, '....while the fire was raging, bingo enthusiasts were helping to shift the equipment, books and prizes to the Hippodrome, ready for the following evening's session.'

Opened on July 14th 1913, the Palace was the town's first purpose built cinema and was erected on a site that had been the centre courtyard of the Royal Livery Stables which was once the mews of the *Royal Hotel*. Indeed, much of the old mews were left standing and the theatre was flanked on two sides by the old stables.

The first film to be shown there was 'Les Miserables', a masterpiece of its time and was the first of many films to be shown at the cinema which was open for over fifty years. Like all cinemas though, the Palace was hard hit by the coming of television and only a few months before the fire, bingo had taken the place of films.

The building was left in a derelict condition until it was finally demolished in March 1971, although a small part of it was saved and used for a while as an auction room.

The Grand was originally built as a swimming pool, fitted with a pipe which led to the sea so that the pool could have fresh seawater. After the First World War the Grand was converted, with the original pool still under the floor, and re-opened as a cinema showing its first film in 1920, a 'moving drama' called 'Nobody's Child'. The cinema had 1,000 seats and a glass roof which was lavishly advertised as admitting "...sea air and sunshine, nature's disinfectants."

The Grand gamely fought the arrival of television with a series of foreign and 3D films but in the 1960s finally succumbed and was turned into a bingo hall, pictured here in 1980. Recently the building has been empty and fell into a state of disrepair but it is currently being renovated, with the whole of its frontage being demolished and rebuilt.

The Ideal Cinema in Norwich Road was opened by a Mr. 'Dickie' Bird in the mid-1930s. The building had originally been a Methodist Chapel built in 1872, but was converted by Mr. Bird who had been showing films in an old net store at the back of Hervey Street. The cinema closed during the Second World War, never to re-open, and although the building was used as a furniture store for some time, it is still standing with the rusted beams attached to the building's facade which once boasted the cinema's name.

The demolition of Sparrow's Nest in 1991. When the Marina closed in 1985 it left the town without a single cinema, leading to a long and hard fought struggle as Waveney District Council wavered between buying and restoring the Marina or refurbishing Sparrow's Nest.

The Nest theatre had been a problem for the council since the navy pulled out after the War. They wanted a more centralised theatre and in 1952 were on the verge of buying the Playhouse (now the Hollywood), as a replacement for the Sparrow's Nest. However, the £10,000 deal fell through when the building was inundated with floods in January 1953 and it was bought by comedian Roy Barbour instead for £11,000. Ten years later the council had another chance to buy the same theatre for just £12,000 but had cold feet again.

In 1986 when the Council finally opted to renovate the Marina instead this spelt the end for the Sparrow's Nest and in September 1988, as the Marina re-opened with a Rick Wakeman concert, the Nest faced the final curtain. Singer Joe Brown played to a near full house, with plenty of local dignitaries paying their last respects to the old theatre. "It's good to see they've come to the funeral!" Joe Brown quipped.

For a while there was talk of converting the theatre but in 1991 the building was finally demolished and the town lost one of its most famous landmarks.

Promises for a new bridge had been made and broken regularly in the years prior to the old swing bridge's demise, such as in 1961 when assurances were made that work would start on a new structure in 1965. In 1967 it was announced that the bridge house, the sewage pumping station, Thain's shop and restaurant and the Yarmouth stores would all need to be demolished for the construction of a new bridge and it was hoped that work would begin at the end of 1968. It never did though and in January 1969 the old swing bridge jammed in the open position and threw the town into chaos. Now there was no alternative. Traffic was sent on a five mile excursion, enormous queues built up, traders lost business and there was even the threat of a one day strike. One man even swam across the harbour to get across the river and was promptly fined £1.

First an emergency footbridge was hastily supplied by the army, followed by a swing footbridge and then a temporary retractable structure, which is shown in the picture below being put into place in March 1970. Large blocks of concrete were lowered into position to act as counterweights on Lowestoft's 215 foot temporary bridge. In fact this structure was four foot wider than the old swing bridge which meant that big vehicles such as lorries and buses could actually pass each other on the bridge for the first time.

The photograph on the right was taken by Gordon Steward from the top of a crane. It was taken on Friday April 17th, 1970, and shows Lowestoft's old swing bridge being swung for the last time before work began on its demolition. On the bridge for its last crossing were Mr R. Owen (Docks Manager), Captain J. Green (Harbour Master) and Mr J. Mc Kinnon (Docks Board Foreman).

Either side of the swing bridge can be seen two of its replacements, with the emergency footbridge now redundant and the temporary retractable bridge now carrying Lowestoft's pedestrians and traffic.

One landmark which disappeared to make way for the new bridge, but is still standing in the photograph, was 'Round House', which had been occupied for 65 years by Craskes who moved a few yards to No. 4 Pier Terrace. When the old swing bridge was dismantled, a new temporary sliding bridge was put in its place while a new double-leaf bascule bridge was built by its side. Finally, after all this disruption, Lowestoft's new bridge was opened in March 1972 by James Prior M.P.

The *Frederick Edward Crick* was Lowestoft's lifeboat from 1963 to 1987 and is shown here in a choppy sea with Jack Rose aboard, second from the left. This lifeboat was a forty-seven foot Watson cabin boat fitted with two 60hp Gardiner diesels and cost £40,000.

In the 1980s the boat suffered technical problems and was twice withdrawn from service for long periods. Soon it was announced that she would be replaced with another boat and her last launch was on the 29th January, 1986 and a few days later she went up to Fletcher's yard and was sold out of service to Southend owners as the *Helen Christina*. A temporary lifeboat took her place at the station until the arrival of the forty-seven foot Tyne boat *Spirit of Lowestoft* in November 1987. She was named this because the money to buy her was raised by the people of the town.

Lowestoft fish market circa 1960. In 1963 a £500,000 scheme for improving the fish market was mooted and the town had to wait until the mid-1980s when a £1.5 million facelift of the fish market was announced. This included the construction of a new auction hall and fish processing area in addition to the improvement of existing facilities and in September 1987 the new fish market was opened by John McGregor M.P.

The improvement work also involved the demolition of all the fish sheds which are shown stretching into the distance on the left of the photo. However, two of these market sheds were lifted by crane and handed over to the Excelsior Sailing Trust to provide an authentic quayside setting for other relics of the age of sail.

Since its re-opening the fish market is now the venue of a bi-annual Fish Fayre which has been such a success that consideration is now being given to making it an annual event.

Over the years there have been many different kinds of catches brought into Lowestoft's fish market and here, in 1938, tuna fish are being loaded onto a fish merchant's cart.

The buildings in the background are on Battery Green and to the left can be seen the Salvation Army hostel.

The old steam drifters that once lined Lowestoft harbour are now only a memory.
Pictured here on the west side of Waveney Dock in the 1950s is the steam drifter *Golden Ring* LT408, which was originally the *Lasher* KY25, and was eventually broken up in April 1957 at Bruges in Belgium.

The *Gas House Tavern* stood in Wilde Street, near Cumberland Square and was one of thirteen public houses in the beach village. A long established pub, the earliest record of it goes back to 1855 and this tavern was one of the last buildings left standing in the beach area before it too was demolished in October 1967.

The *Rising Sun* stood on the corner of Spurgeon Street and Whapload Road and was affectionately known by locals as the 'Japanese Embassy'. Many believe that the 1953 flood was the last straw for the beach village as it left many of the properties in the area uninhabitable and by the end of the 1960s the area had been cleared.

Looking down Rant Score in the early 1960s. In the distance can be seen the top of the gasworks, and on the right the little cottages that were soon to be demolished.

St. Peter's Cottage could be found in St. Peter's Street. The opening by its side lead to Bemments Buildings, cottages that were demolished in the mid-1960s, around the same time that St. Peter's Cottage was knocked down too.

The site of Smith's Cottages in the Hemplands is today part of busy Jubilee Way. This was the oldest part of the town and although it was home to some interesting architecture, it has to be said that some of the living conditions were very bad and some of the buildings should have been condemned long before they were. It seems likely that another reason why improvement work wasn't forthcoming was because of the new road system which had been in the pipeline for many years.

The company of Rist's Wire and Cables Ltd. was owned by Mr. Albert Rist, and supplied electrical parts for Model-T Fords. Mr. Rist at one time lived in the mansion of Normanhurst which was demolished in the early 1970s and stood on the site of the present fire station. The company of Rist's left the town in the late 1930s.

In September 1967 Lowestoft lost one of its landmarks when this water tower in School
Road was demolished. The four clover-shaped tanks were to catch and store rainwater for
the Alliance Artificial Silk Company who built the tower after moving into a factory near
this site around 1930. By 1936 the company had closed and during the War the tower
was used as a naval training base. In 1951 TV Manufacturing took over the silk factory
buildings and mounted aerials on the tower for a radio link with their head office in
Cambridge. However, by the time the tower was taken down it had been disused for
sometime.

TV Manufacturing began with just twenty employees producing a simple radio receiver,
and gradually increased its workforce, developing the area around the factory to become
an important part of the town's economy. Eventually though, business slumped and in the
early 1980s Sanyo saved the company from extinction and today is once more among the
biggest employers in the town.

In 1936 another silkworks, Hinde Fras. & Sons Ltd, was established at Oulton Broad in
Victoria Road and during the War produced thousand of yards of fabric for parachutes,
barrage balloons, dinghies and life-saving jackets. In the 1950s production switched to
fabrics for dresses, typewriter ribbons and curtains. In 1962 the company re-organised
and extended its main Norwich factory and closed the Oulton works, making eighty-two
people redundant, and silk was no longer made in Oulton Broad.

The closure of the former CWS canning factory on October 14th 1994 came as a complete shock to all concerned. The closure was announced at noon on that black Friday and staff were given just fifteen minutes to leave. 350 jobs were lost.

This comes just a few months after Richard's shipbuilders announced its closure in May 1994 with the loss of 40 jobs - Richard's employed 500 people at its Lowestoft and Yarmouth yards during the 1980s but it had been shedding its workforce due to decreasing orders.

The closure of the canning factory is the latest in an ever-increasing list of long established companies which have been forced to close in the last ten years. Among them are Eastern Coachworks, Morton's, Bally shoe factory and Brooke Yachts.

SECTION 2

Through The Streets

A bird's eye view of the town, just after the War. The beach and harbour are the most prominent places on view while the old Reading Room, demolished in 1954, can be seen on the South Pier. Towards the centre of the photograph can also be seen the Beach Village which at this time was still heavily populated. The tree-lined road on the far left is in fact Clapham Road and is just one of the many places of interest that can be picked out if you study this captivating photograph of how Lowestoft was.

Early view of Lowestoft Esplanade, showing the old wooden pier and reading room which was destroyed by fire on the 29th June 1885, causing an estimated £8,000 worth of damage.

On the right can be seen one of the two Triton statues, both of which are still standing, the other one being sited on the seafront opposite the Hatfield Hotel. These were sculpted in the 1850s as part of Peto's striking terrace and were given a facelift in 1961 after many years of standing up to the sand, sea spray and wind. In 1983 the statue in the photograph needed further restoration work that involved re-cutting the figure's details which had become blurred and worn down. At the time it was discovered that there was no mason's mark on the statue, which is unusual, so the sculptor of the two Tritons sadly remains anonymous.

Triton is half man, half dolphin and was the son of Neptune. Usually he is depicted holding a shell trumpet, his job being to blow it at Neptune's command, to soothe the restless waves of the sea. However the Lowestoft Tritons are holding cornucopias, the horn of plenty, disgorging fruit of a rich variety. It does seem odd though that a sea god should have been able to get hold of such a lot of fruit!

The Playhouse in London Road South. There has been a long history of entertainments on this site. Originally an auctioneer's sale room with offices at the front, this building was converted into a dance hall and then into a theatre by Mr. F.C. Symonds, a local estate agent. Known as the 'New Theatre', in 1927 Symonds renamed it the 'Playhouse' with repertory companies putting on plays there. However, when the Grand showed the first 'talkie' in the town in 1929 with a film called 'Sonny Boy', it wasn't long before the Playhouse followed and about a year later showed their first film, 'Broadway Melody'.

The Playhouse survived the War but burned down in June 1946 and was rebuilt, opening two years later as the 'New Playhouse'. Following Mr. Symonds' death, his wife sold the concern to north country comedian Roy Barbour in 1952. Barbour renamed it the 'Arcadia' and put on a summer show, followed by repertory, a pantomime and films. Suffering from the advent of television, in 1959 the Arcadia was taken over by Noel Gay productions who held a competition to find another new name for the place. Among the suggestions were 'The Bridge', 'Neptune', 'The Rising Sun' and 'Kipperdrome' but the new owners plumped for the 'Theatre Royal'. Subsequently a series of plays were put on but it soon became apparent that the new Theatre Royal was not going to be a success and it was sold to Mr. Roy Dashwood in 1962 and following the vogue of the day it became the 'Royal Casino' bingo hall. It remained this until the late 1980s when Mr. Trevor Wicks re-converted the building, transforming it into a modern 460 seat cinema. Re-named 'The Hollywood' it re-opened on 30th November 1989 with a charity performance of 'Ghostbusters II' and the old 'Playhouse', seven names later and over seventy years since it was first a cinema, had a new lease of life.

Looking down London Road South towards the bridge after the War. The bricked-up area on the right with the trees was once a doctor's house and grounds but in August 1957 the area was cleared and the Marine Parade filling station was built in its place.

A 'bridger' with a difference. On one occasion just after the War, as traffic waited for a boat to pass through the opened bridge, it didn't! The unfortunate vessel was stuck for some time and presumably frayed the nerves of many drivers and pedestrians before it was finally moved.

The South Pier in its glory days before the Second World War. During the War years the bandstand was bombed and the crowns on the pier's entrance were taken down. When the entrance to the pier was removed, one of the kiosks was restored and re-sited by the miniature railway near the south beach, while another sat rotting away for ten years at the Corporation depot and became a piece of ornate nineteenth century firewood.

On the end of the pier can be seen the old Reading Room, built between 1888 and 1891 which stood until May 1954 when it was replaced with a less attractive structure which was opened by the Duke of Edinburgh in 1956. This in turn was demolished in January 1989, cleared to make way for a redevelopment scheme involving the Yacht Club.

The view from the bridge, looking south in 1994. At the top of the photo can be seen the lane signals which were introduced in the late 1980s enabling the lanes' priorities to be changed during the busier and slacker times of the day.

Levington Court can also be seen in the background of the photograph, built on the site of St. John's church.

A carnival and regatta day in the 1920s. The origins of the carnival are unsure but it seems likely that some kind of event has taken place in Lowestoft since the turn of the century. The official programme of 'Lowestoft's five day carnival' in 1924 boasts of a "...procession of decorated private and trade vehicles and cycles." The five day event received national press coverage and was held from July 8th to 12th, 1924. The carnival opened with an historical re-enactment of the landing of King George II who then delegated his powers of suzerainty to the carnival king and queen whom he crowned. Judging by the publicity given to it - the event had a centre spread in the Daily Mirror - the Lowestoft Carnival wasn't just a local event that year.

The yacht basin in the 1960s, showing the old swing bridge in close proximity to the harbour-master's cottage. On the north side of the bridge, the small white building was Thain's restaurant which could be found at the back of Thain's fishmongers shop. These were all pulled down for the construction of the new bridge in the early 1970s.

The Royal Norfolk and Suffolk Yacht Club building on the left is one of the few buildings in the town that have Grade II listed status. Among the others are the Town Hall, Denes High School, the two Triton statues by the seafront and Wellington Esplanade which was only recognised in 1993. Also listed is the Victorian semi-detached house on Kirkley Cliff where Benjamin Britten grew up.

31

Looking towards 'Suffolk Corner' at Christmas in the late 1950s. The white building opposite Barclays Bank was a taxi rank while to the left of the *Suffolk Hotel* can be seen the *Imperial Hotel*.

Station Square in the early 1920s. The buildings that can be seen in front of the railway station housed shops, among them Buck's sweetshop, and when they were finally demolished in 1929, due to increasing traffic, an island was built here where the buses stopped.
   Over the years there have been various traffic systems in this area and various names too, among them United Corner (after the United Automobile Services parcel office which was situated here in the 1920s) and Suffolk Corner although since the late 1970s the area has been known as Station Square.

The railway station, one of Lowestoft's earliest buildings, was built in the 1850s by the Lucas Brothers. Pictured here in 1978, at this time it remained largely in its original state but since then its condition has sadly deteriorated leading to the controversial proposal of its demolition being announced in the early 1990s. The station was saved, but its roof has been removed due to its poor condition. Despite a new reception area, today the station looks like a crumbling ruin at the very entrance to the town, which one day will presumably be given as the reason for finally knocking it down completely.

Looking down Denmark Road in the early 1960s. On the right can be seen the neat gardens of the *Imperial Hotel*, while the trees were only removed in the mid-70s for road widening.

Denmark Road was once known as the harbour village because of all the fishermen's houses in the area, an alternative to the beach village. It was named after one of the many cattle ships that came to the town in the nineteenth century.

Looking down Bevan Street in the 1960s with the *Imperial Hotel* and *Suffolk Hotel* at the entrance of the road. The property at the furthest end of Bevan Street was demolished to make way for the new road in the 1970s.

For most of the nineteenth century this street was known as Chapel Lane but a change of name was requested by property owners in June 1871. Alma Road was one popular suggestion while Bevan Street was suggested presumably because, at one time, a Bevan Estate was in this area. When it came to the vote there were seven votes for and seven against and it was the chairman who had the casting vote - and Bevan Street it was.

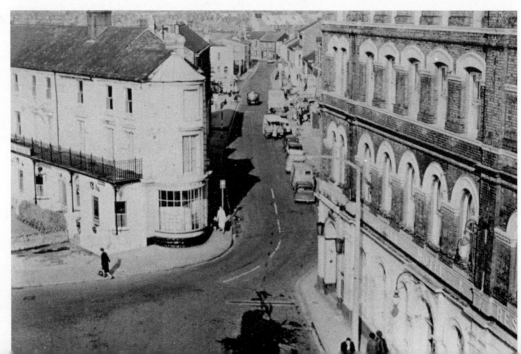

The *Imperial Hotel*, which was situated on the corner of Denmark Road. This hotel was originally built as a row of terrace houses though subsequently these premises were used as shops. Henry Tuttle was among the retailers situated here before the building was converted into *Foulsham's Railway Hotel* in the early 1900s. In 1941 an underground toilet outside the hotel received a direct hit from a German bomb and a number of people were killed and over half the hotel demolished. After this, the *Imperial* was never used again as a hotel, the upstairs rooms were sealed off, and the downstairs was a public house. The last manager of the hotel, Mr. Cyril Bidle, went on record as saying that no-one had set foot in those bedrooms since that day in 1941 until the demolition men arrived thirty years later!

In 1972 the old *Imperial Hotel* was redeveloped and partly rebuilt and the premises converted back into shops.

This photograph can be dated by the fact that Chilver's is still standing in the row of shops, next to the lamp-post. These premises were rendered derelict by a bomb blast in 1941 but weren't demolished until 1953 when new premises were built for the Eastern Gas Board. On the right is the *Spread Eagle* which has since been called the *Carousel* and is today the *Wheatsheaf*.

Wesley House in the High Street was built in the mid-1980s on the site of the Wesleyan Chapel. The architecture of these flats obviously contained more than a hint of the old chapel which was built in 1862 in an Italian style from designs by Mr. John Louth Clemence and can be seen below.

In January 1969 the Methodist Church had been sold to Hughes for £12,500 and used as a television maintenance and distribution centre, although services were still held there until May 1970. When Hughes took over the building it soon proved unsuitable and within a few years they vacated the premises which remained empty until its demolition in May 1984.

Another link with Lowestoft's past is the crest which sits proudly on the front of Wesley House which was saved from the *Royal Hotel*.

Looking east towards the North Post Office in the High Street in the early 1960s. Green's the printers was on the right and the premises with the bow window was the shop owned by Mrs. Bagshaw. The shop by the lamppost was Hawkes the hairdressers and on the left of the street was Crown Stores and the Rose & Crown Public House. All this property was demolished for Jubilee Way.

View of the High Street in the mid-1950s. *The Anchor Hotel* on the left is now occupied by *Bayfields*. The large building on the right was once the Seaview Temperance Hotel, while next to it were premises which housed a pawnbrokers originally run by Mr. William Scarlett. When Robert Smith took over he also bought the adjoining temperance hotel from where he ran a furnishing business. In 1940 these buildings suffered bomb damage causing Mr. Smith to transfer his business to 38 London Road North and the High Street was without a pawnbroker for the first time in over a century. Subsequently these buildings were left derelict, as they are in the photograph, until they were demolished in February 1957 and the site was cleared, giving passers-by a different view of the sea. Eventually new shops were built and the corner site is now occupied by a Chinese take-away.

Lowestoft has lost many quirky buildings but not always for new roads or because of their own disrepair. Demolition work began in late 1963 on these houses adjoining Arnold House, Nos.7, 9 & 10 High Street, due to damage caused by lightning in the early 1960s.

Belle Vue Park, pictured here early this century, was opened on 28th March 1874 by the Lord and Lady of the Manor, Mr. and Mrs. Robert Reeve.

   The cannons to the left of the picture were placed there for ornamentation when the park opened but during the War were put away for safe keeping and buried. Unfortunately they were forgotten and eventually were dug up in 1971 at the Corporation depot in Rotterdam Road. They were in a poor condition but they were restored and replaced in the park.

At the time of the photo in the early 1900s, the north beach was popular with the people living at this end of the town who had no need to cross the bridge to play in the sand. Once, between the sea and the Denes were the 'Marram Hills', named after the marram grass which grew there and held together the sand that was gradually being washed away. It seems hard now to believe, but there was a beach beyond Ness Point, where Jack remembers, "..... as children we would search for amber, which we could sell for a few bob to Camp's Antiques...."

In addition to this, between the North and South Denes was a model yacht pond, opened in July 1889, which continued in use until just after the Second World War. In winter, when the water was frozen, skating took place, and fancy dress carnivals would be held. At night the pond would even be illuminated by Chinese lanterns! There was also skating on the rough ice on the South Denes when the temperature dropped low enough to freeze the high tides.

Over the years the north beach was greatly reduced in width owing to coastal erosion and every time a sea wall was built it was inundated by the sea. Now the area has been given over to industry.

The vast mural on Boston Deep Sea Fisheries in Waveney Road was made at the same time as the offices in 1905 and depicts Columbus's Fleet.

Special hollow bricks were supplied by Dalton & Cockerill to make the design and though there were fears at the time that the mural would not stand up to the weather, it is still intact ninety years later.

Shopping

London Road North in 1951

Home Services in London Road South was opened after the last War by Mr. Donald Morgan, whose brother Doug played the piano at the South Pier. The second-hand shop only had a brief life though, and closed in the mid-1950s.

SHOPPING IN LOWESTOFT

To the visitor one of the first impressions of a town are the shops they find within it. Shops help give a town its identity and Lowestoft is no exception. In the past the town has boasted independent stores such as Tuttle's, Catling's, Hailey's and Pryce's, and even today still has a smattering of old family businesses such as Chadd's, Jarrold's, Morling's and Bushell's. These are long established firms, managing to survive in the era of the multiple store when every town centre is in danger of becoming indistinguishable from the next.

The cosy feel of shopping has gone. Once upon a time at Christmas it was the custom to parade the streets and compare the decorated shop windows. Shops would vye with each other to make the best displays of their particular wares, using everything from flower displays to clockwork figures. The atmosphere has altered now, Christmas become coldly commercialised, but once shops were individual and their owners were often characters who played a big role in the community.

Lilians in London Road South. There had been a drapers in these premises, 202 London Road South, probably since the building was erected. Around the turn of this century F.R. Freeman had a drapery store there followed by a Mr. Fred Owers. He was succeeded by Dagley and Son's who called themselves 'general drapers' but by 1930 the shops had passed into the hands of Alf Bunguard. After the War a Miss Lilian Spink took over the premises, naming the shop Lilians and over the coming years the shop's reputation grew. In the 1960s Chadd's took over the store but it kept the name 'Lilians' until its closure in 1990.

In 1952 Lowestoft had 824 shops, that was one for every 53 people, and it is interesting to see just how many different stores there were, many of which today have been absorbed into one big shop:

Grocers	78	Jewellers	10
Cafes & restaurants	48	Tailors	10
Fruiterers & greengrocers	46	Stationers	9
Butchers	44	Wool	9
Confectioners	38	Opticians	8
Fried fish	33	Photographers	7
Boot & shoe repairs	29	Ironmongers	7
Gents' hairdressers	29	Corn chandlers	6
Ladies' hairdressers	25	Printers	6
Shoe shops	24	Dyers & cleaners	5
Bakers	24	Fancy goods	5
Newsagents	24	Florists	5
Drapers	20	Antique dealers	4
Outfitters	19	Booksellers	4
Cycle shops	18	Hardware	4
Fishmongers	18	Ships' chandlers	4
Tobacconists	17	Secondhand goods	4
Chemists	17	Sports outfitters	3
House furnishers	13	Saddlers	3
Dairies	12	Hosiery repair	3
Electrical engineers	12	Gown shops	3
Radio	12	Multiple stores	2
Wines & spirits	10	Unclassified	90

Lowestoft is now home to many discount stores but perhaps the first of its kind in the town was 'Brenner's 1d Bazaar' which was originally located at 121 Bevan Street just before the First World War. It had a brief life there and moved to larger premises in London Road North next to Regent Road. Both shops were open-fronted arcades with counters around three sides, and when closed were secured by wooden shutters, operated roller-blind fashion. Brenner's eventually gave way to rivals and the premises were taken over by Halford's although the name Brenner's could be seen in the mosaic paving of the shop doorway long after the the Second World War.

While the penny bazaar was certainly an innovation, and not without a mixed reception from local traders, there was another very popular bazaar in existence well before then, the old 'sixpenny-ha'penny bazaar' in the premises later occupied by Timothy White's, now Millet's, in London Road North. They dealt with glass and china of reasonably good quality though the price was rigidly applied so a cup and saucer would cost one shilling and a penny. This company eventually moved to the north of the town, just below the Victorian Arcade, before going out of business.

Bevan Street was always a brisk trading area and can probably lay claim to having had the town's first supermarket. Nos. 12, 13, 14 & 15 were owned by Mr. John Wade Bond who owned a family business in the early 1900s. Although separate shops, they were all linked by archways in the walls, thus providing a clear walk through although retaining their individual shop doorways. It was possible to enter No. 12, devoted to ironmongery, wallpaper and hardware, pass through to No. 13 for dolls, toys, books, stationery and newspapers, which led to drapery and household linen in No. 14, and finally millinery and dresses at No. 15. Most goods were displayed on shelves and each department had its own counter and cash till.

After the Second World War London Road North had many gaps to fill due to the bombing. In the 1950s and 60s the town centre was gradually rebuilt and by the 1970s there were very few plum sites left. One of the last 'undeveloped' sites was the Baptist Church which for many years had been a target for developers and it finally succumbed in 1972 when it was demolished and Boot's new shop was built there. That left only the Prairie, which became the site of the £11 million Britten Centre, opened in 1987.

The new market place that opened within the Britten Centre however only served to deplete the Triangle Market in the High Street. This market had been first established in 1898, only temporarily, on a site that had been bought for the new town hall. However, the cost of this project was considered so outrageous that the plans were dropped and the temporary market area was cleared and planted with shrubs and flowers. In the meantime the market had become popular with the townspeople and the clearance of the site sparked a storm of protest, with angry housewives tearing up the bushes and flowers and ripping up the fencing. They even built a huge bonfire on which they burned an effigy of a leading councillor. For once the council backed down and the Triangle Market stayed.

The market and town hall seem to be inextricably linked in Lowestoft as when the plans for the Britten Centre were drawn up it was suggested that the town hall and all its departments were incorporated within the new construction. However, these plans were dropped.

The pedestrianisation of the London Road North shopping area is probably the most dramatic change in shopping in Lowestoft since the War. It has at least taken away the traffic fumes and made it a little safer for the shopper but pedestrianisation has proved impractical at times. Security vehicles and delivery lorries still have to visit shops and banks in the area, as there is no other way to get to some premises, and they have to drive on the 'pedestrianised' area. Another problem is that London Road North is actually a continuous incline right up to the High Street. This makes walking from the bottom of London Road North (or London Road South) to the High Street quite a long and weary journey and where you

Thain's Fishmongers was an old-established name in the town at its site opposite Pier Terrace and behind these premises could be found Thain's restaurant. The fishmongers were never short of advertising ideas as the window shows in the photograph. It suggests that the customer should, ".....send your friends a box of bloaters and kippers...."

In the same row of shops as Thain's, most people would remember these premises being occupied by Yarmouth Stores, where fishermen obtained all their gear, which opened just before the First World War. This little row of three shops were demolished to make way for the new bridge in the early 1970s.

could once hop on a bus or pull up outside a shop in a car, now you have to walk there or drive round the one way system. The response to this has been the arrival of the many 'superstores' such as Tesco's in Gunton and the North Quay Industrial Park which have the attraction of shoppers being able to drive right up to the door of the shop. Of course, the arrival of out-of-town stores does have an effect on the shops left behind, taking trade away from the town centre.

The length of London Road has long been a problem and there have been many attempts to break it up. As early as 1926 there was a campaign mounted for the renaming of the top end of London Road North to 'The Broadway'. Some local businessmen were so confident of the change that they even had their letterheads reprinted! Other suggestions for the road's new name were Central Road or Central Avenue but nothing was ever done. Rival suggestions proved too much for the council who decided it was better left as it was!

London Road South still has to cope with the busy A12 traffic too but the flip-side to this is the passing trade it brings with it and being able to park outside the shops. The Bridge Road traders in Oulton Broad relied on this though and have suffered as a result of being bypassed by a new road in the early 1990s while in 1993 the High Street shops suffered a similar fate with the construction of Artillery Way. Sometimes it seems people forget these secondary shopping areas, but these are where the smaller independent traders are found today, shops that give Lowestoft an identity however much it changes.

Mr. James Garrod was Lowestoft's last surviving saddle and harness maker. Situated at 16 Bevan Street, he was in business until the late 1960s when the premises became a saddle boutique.

The Walker Regis shop near the bridge, pictured in 1977 celebrating the Queen's Jubilee. Selling gifts and travel goods, Walker Regis became one of Lowestoft's most famous independent shops since the last War.

Established by Reg Walker, an agent for a leather goods manufacturer and Reg Regis, owner of a sports shop in London Road South, the partnership's first shop was opened on November 22nd 1947 in premises next to Barclays Bank in London Road North.

By the mid-50s Reg Regis had left the partnership although the name Walker-Regis remained and in 1964 when the bank closed, the shop expanded into these premises. In addition to this, Reg Walker opened another shop in London Road North and two 'Leather Luxe' shops, one in London Road South and the other within the premises of the Odeon Cinema. This building was sold to W.H. Smith in 1972 and Leather Luxe moved to 2-4 Denmark Road and formed part of Reg Walker's new shop 'Century 21', opening on November 25th 1972.

In September 1991 despite assurances from the council, the busy road outside the London Road North shop was now making it difficult for people to get there. Tony Walker, Reg's son, decided to close and relocate to his own premises on the corner of Denmark Road, keeping alive the famous Walker-Regis name.

In August 1972 the site of the former *Suffolk Hotel* was redeveloped at a cost of £150,000 and this picture, taken in 1974, shows the new Lipton's shop near to completion.
Lipton's had opened their first self-service store in the town near Woolworth's some years after the last War but this new shop in Station Square closed just nine years after it was opened, in December 1983, when the premises were turned into a fast food restaurant.

Fielding's opened after the last War at No. 75 London Road North and is shown here in the 1950s with a display of bicycles. This shop closed in the late 1960s and the premises were taken over by Halford's who remained there until 1993, when they opened a large warehouse on the new North Quay Shopping Park.

By the 1980s most of the town's shopping area had been developed. This picture, taken in 1980 shows the Odeon no longer with us and a pedestrianised London Road North as Lowestoft began to attract some of the bigger chain stores.

London Road North in the 1950s as the Odeon gets a facelift. On the left can be seen another of the town's most notable independent shops, Craik's fruiterers and provisions. Mr. Craik was in business as a photographer but decided to switch to the confectionery trade and in 1926 he and his wife opened a shop in Bevan Street. About four years later Mrs. Craik opened the London Road North shop selling high-class fruit, cakes and confectionery but as there were other greengrocers in the area they did not deal in this trade.

Shortly before the War the Bevan Street shop was sold, Mrs. Craik retired and Mr. Craik took over the London Road shop. He remained open during the War but the premises were badly damaged by bombing and for about six months Mr. Craik switched the business to the old Bevan Street property again which was vacant at that time. In 1955 the shop was completely rebuilt and extended so that the property entirely covered the rear garden. The stock was greatly enlarged and its reputation was acknowledged throughout the town. In May 1968, owing in some part to the changing nature of shopping, Craik's were forced to close a forty year old business which locals still remember fondly.

A busy London Road North in the late 1950s. The Eastern Counties Omnibus station office on the left of the photo was demolished in 1987 and turned into retail premises which took a small part of the Woolworth's store too.

Catling's was another of Lowestoft's notable independent stores of the past. In June 1964 the company was taken over by Chadd's before it was eventually closed in the early 1980s. The premises were demolished and a new Fine Fare shop built and opened, which has since been renamed Gateway and is now Somerfields.

56

In 1964 Tesco's opened their new supermarket in the town, the chain store's first on this part of the coast. To make way for this new development Curtis's restaurant, one of Lowestoft's best known buildings, was demolished in November 1963. There had been a restaurant in these premises for more than fifty years and it was one of the oldest properties in London Road North having once been a doctor's home and a dentist's surgery.

London Road North in the 1980s with the new Tesco's shop on the left. This decade saw Tesco's redeveloped again, demolishing the three shops to their left and their own original store to build new premises to their own requirements. In the early 1990s there were fears that Tesco's would abandon their town centre shop in preference for their new store which was opened on the outskirts of the town in Gunton. However, at the moment the London Road shop remains.

The Arcade was built around the turn of the century on land where the old Baptist Church had stood, which today would be near the site of the Journal Office. Before the War the occupants were a florist who could be found at Nos. 1, 2 and 3, at No. 4 was an upholsterer and other traders included a baker and a brush manufacturer. The British Legion Club was also in the Arcade which was destroyed in a bombing raid during the last War.

The old Journal Office was built in 1872 and was the only building in this row to survive the wartime bombing. In the mid-1960s a new property was built at the rear of these premises and the Journal Office and Walker's stores were demolished to correct the building line, with the Journal relocating to the new building behind it.

Fletcher's the butchers and the Weaver's leather shop, Nos. 171 and 173 London Road North. These two shops were alongside each other from the 1920s for around forty years before Weaver's finally closed in the late 1960s and the premises were acquired by fruiterers. Fletcher's continued trading until the mid-1960s when they were taken over by Dewhurst's.

The High Street and Triangle Market after the widening of the St. Peter's Street junction in 1962 which reduced the size of the market. This resulted in fewer stalls and those that remained had to move to new positions.

Devereux's shop, seen at the back of the photo, was built on the site that was once let to a travelling waxwork show, which also included a lion-faced woman and a glass blower. It was reported at the time that the lion-faced woman did have a yellowish face but succeeded only in making the audience uncomfortable and most people were relieved at the appearance of the glass blower!

A row of shops in St. Peter's Street in the late 1970s. On the left is John Gall's the hair-dressers, where the famous 'Cunningham's Clock' can be seen in the window.

The clock was probably installed in 1887 when the firm of Cunningham's watchmakers and jewellers first opened here. It had to be accurate because it was a clockmaker's sign, and over the years became a reliable friend to all clockwatchers in the town. After the last War Cunningham's moved to Halesworth and it was thought that they had taken the clock with them. It left a noticeable hole though and in 1950 when John Gall the hairdresser opened in these premises, so persistent were the enquiries as to the clock's whereabouts that he decided to search for a replacement and found one in an Oulton Broad shop. Two weeks later though Mr. Gall heard that the original clock was in the possession of the Liverpool Victoria Insurance Co., who owned the building, and when he told them the story they let him have the clock back.

The clock remained in its place in the window for another thirty-five years, but when John Gall finally closed around the mid-1980s, the clock disappeared again. Where this ancient timepiece is today has not been disclosed.

Bingham's Restaurant and Coffee House was a favourite among locals, opening in the early 1930s in premises that were once another of the town's public houses, belonging to the company of Lowestoft Beachmen. Bingham's closed in the mid-1970s and today the building is an Italian restaurant. On the left can be seen Panda Books, which opened in 1973 and four years later expanded into bigger premises further down at 117 High Street where they still are today.

The Co-operative Society's premises in Clapham Road were almost completely destroyed during the first air-raid of the the War on July 3rd 1940. After the bombing the Co-op hired, and later bought, the premises of Parker and Watson Ltd, a firm of drapers, in the High Street and moved their drapery, outfitting and boot departments there in addition to their men's shop. However, the High Street shop, as shown in the photograph, did not come through the War unshaken and parts of the building were badly damaged and could not be used at all. In March 1956 the property was reduced to ground level and rebuilt entirely, with the Co-op moving to 61-67 London Road North during its construction. In November 1956 the shop opened in the new High Street building, which was described as 'continental' in style. The Co-op remained in these premises until the mid-1960s and more recently the building has been occupied by the Mart and Allen's Music but is currently empty.

Percy Wigg opened a furnishing shop after the Second World War in Brett's old premises on the corner of Duke's Head Street and the High Street. In addition to this Percy Wigg's were a removal and storage contractor and also had premises in Bridge Road, Oulton Broad and a coal and coke merchants business in St. Peter's Street. In the early 1980s Percy Wigg retired and the business closed. Currently the Duke's Head Street premises is a restaurant.

P. Coleby's fruiterer and florist was another long established name. The Colebys took over the shop from Ms. E. Soons in the late 1930s and ran the business for over forty years. An attempt was made to get the ornate doors of the old shop listed and they are still intact today, with the building now being occupied by an opticians.

Wymer's paper shop at 133 Duke's Head Street was previously owned by a Mr. Hubbard whose father was one of the Lowestoft town-criers. This paper shop was one of many little shops at the north end of town and was demolished as part of the clearance of the area in the mid-1960s.

Ronnie Cook's was a family butchery business which was in the town for almost sixty years. Mr. Ronnie Cook was born in Whapload Road, where his father Sidney Cook had been in business as a butcher for two years. In 1928 S. Cook and Son Ltd opened in Bevan Street, and it was from there that Mr. Ronnie Cook came to High Street.

Later the shop was passed down to Ronnie's son Roger who took the decision to close in October 1985, blaming the closure on supermarkets taking trade, a change in eating habits and a new road system which stopped the flow of passing trade.

Here are the histories of some of Lowestoft's longest established firms, past and present, big and small....

BUSHELL'S BAKERY

Bushell's is the town's longest serving bakery, having first made bread in 1883 in premises in Duke's Head Street. In 1962 this area was re-developed and after over seventy years on the site, the bakery was moved to premises adjacent to the shop in Tennyson Road. In addition to this there were shops in London Road South, Norwich Road, Bridge Road and Oulton Road.

The founder of the business was Mr. Walter Wiseman Bushell who passed the business to his son Walter in 1937. Everything at the Duke's Head Street bakery was made by hand and the bread put in and taken out of the oven at the end of a long shovel. At this time there was only one employee to help although in 1939 Walter's son Peter joined the firm until he was called-up and joined the army. After the War the business expanded and by 1959 they had two vans and the bakery was enlarged. Since 1962 the firm has been run by Peter Bushell but it wasn't until 1969 that his father finally retired.

CHADD'S

Chadd's was founded in 1907 by G.B. Chadd, at 99 London Road North in premises that had previously been the Coronet cinema. G.B. Chadd died in 1940 and after the War when Colonel G.V.N. Chadd returned from active service in the Royal Artillery, he took over control of the business which he greatly expanded. In 1964 Chadd's took over another Lowestoft firm, Catling's while other companies in the group included G.B. Chadd Ltd, Lilian's (Millinery) Ltd, Chadd's Mail Order Wool Ltd, James Ward Ltd in Southwold and Woodland Textiles (Lowestoft) Ltd.

PRYCE'S

This shop first opened in 1897 after the founder Richard Pryce had moved to Lowestoft from Ramsgate. Known as the Lowestoft Hardware Company it was in 1907 that the shop moved across the road to its site in Suffolk Road and over the years gradually acquired premises along the road to extend the store as in 1980 when the shop expanded into the former building of the Library. In 1993 directors John and Robert Pryce announced their retirement and sold the business to Godfrey's.

TUTTLE'S

This firm was started by Henry Tuttle as a grocery and provision store at 66 High Street (until recently the Lowestoft Christian Bookshop). These premises soon became inadequate for the growing business and in 1850 the firm moved to 58 High Street. Five years later in 1855, a branch was opened in Raglan Street and

Inside Tuttle's hosiery and glove department in the mid-50s. Jean Woof can be seen behind the bookstall, while Evelyn Wade and Margaret Warford are behind the cash desk addressed by Queenie Thurston, who supplied this photograph.

soon this had to be abandoned for larger premises at 2 Denmark Road. Here a drapery department was added and when the Grove Estate was developed in the 1880s its famous site was secured and the Bon Marche shop was opened in 1888.

Over the years Tuttle's bought up the little shops alongside them but in 1960 one of Lowestoft's oldest and biggest family concerns was taken over by Debenham's. In July 1972 it was announced that Tuttle's would close on January 27th 1973 but in October 1972 the shop was reprieved when it was bought by Braham's, who already had a shop in London Road South. However, the reprieve was only temporary, and in 1981 the famous Tuttle's sign disappeared and the shop closed for good. For a time the building continued as a department store under the name of Bamber's, but when that closed the building was broken up into smaller shops once again.

TOM BATTRICK, BOOT MAKER

In 1973 the town's oldest established retailing and bespoke boot maker closed down after nearly sixty years of business. Battrick's had been situated in the High Street since 1916, when Tom Battrick came to live in the town. They arrived the very day of the Lowestoft bombardment in April 1916, and Tom kept a piece of shell that he had found red hot after it had dropped just 100 yards from the shop at 81 High Street. In 1935 his son Arthur branched out on his own and set up his own bootmaking business at 175 High Street. In 1943 this shop was bombed, along with the Jubilee Stores, and he moved to temporary premises opposite Coleby's fruiterer and florists where he stayed until his father became ill in 1952 when he returned to the shop where he had learned his trade. At the age of sixty-five in 1973 Arthur Battrick decided to close, as he felt that he could not cope with the paperwork that VAT would cause.

Before he closed he shook the dust off some old stock and made an interesting window display of some old button-up boots and shoes. However, customers started to buy them and button boots that were supposed to be worn with hobble skirts were selling like hot cakes to mini-skirted Lowestoft girls. One young woman bought seventeen pairs! The £1 and 50p price tags might have had something to do with it though!

* * * * *

Morling's was founded in 1892 by Ernest Morling, who gave up his insurance agency to start a small music shop in Old Nelson Street with Mr. Read, a blind piano tuner. As business grew these premises soon proved inadequate and over the coming years Morling's opened other shops.

In the 1930s the firm became a limited company with Ernest as chairman and two sons and two daughters joining him. During the War Morling's shops were bombed twice, Ernest Morling being killed in the Waller's raid on January 13th 1942. As a result the business was transferred to temporary premises at 139 High Street, pictured above. Later in the War tragedy struck again when news was received that Ernest's son Hugh had been killed in the Far East.

After the War Miss Mary Morling, the youngest of Ernest's six children, began to play an active role in the business and in 1954 the company moved back to 149 London Road North. One of Hugh's children, Richard, joined the company in 1970 giving up a promising career in photography to join Aunt Mary in the family business. Mary ran the company till her death in 1981, which was the year that the shop suffered a serious fire too. With Richard Morling in charge, the shop once again rose out of the ashes and was rebuilt and is now one of the oldest established retailers in the town.

The Lowestoft shops of the nineties. Two views of London Road North in 1994 show the town's main shopping centre, looking north (top) and south (bottom). What changes will the reader of the twenty-first century identify in these two photographs?

Townspeople

October 1957 and a large crowd gather in Battery Green to hear the former Prime Minister Lord Attlee deliver a speech.

The girls of the Alderman Woodrow School in 1946-47. Built in the early 1930s, this school was originally set to open in 1932 as the Notley Road School but due to the 'financial stringencies' of the era only part of the project was completed by 1934 when the school opened. A year later five more rooms were added and in 1938 the whole school was finally finished having cost £40,000 and built to accommodate 880 children. Catering for all elder scholars of South Lowestoft and Oulton Broad, the school was divided equally and separately between boys and girls. After the War the school was known as the Alderman Woodrow School, named after John William Woodrow who was Mayor of the town between 1945-47, and the school continued to develop and grow. In the early 1970s it was renamed Kirkley High School as part of the educational changes of the time.

Co-op canteen staff line-up for the camera in the mid-1950s.

The waitresses from the 'New Pakefield Holiday Camp' line-up for the camera in 1953.

Christmas in the late 1950s and some members of staff from Woolworth's in Lowestoft donned their best party clothes and celebrated the season. Back row, left to right: Unknown, Rita Huckle, Mr. Bennett (the manager), Carol Clarke, Sheila Sutton. Front row, Brenda Harvey, Maureen Draper, Margaret Bedwell, Vera ?, Eileen Smith.

A scene from the highlight of the Alderman Woodrow Secondary School's Christmas programme in 1949. This was a mumming play, 'Christmastide' and was told by carols linked by spoken verse and was performed by Form 3P. The angels were: Doreen Disney, Shirley Cone, Beryl Taylor. Also standing, from left to right: Molly Youngs, Pat Dann, Pamela Goldspink, Heather Ayre, Rosemary Fuller, Cynthia Carver. Sitting (centre): Heather Verrall, Rita Wilkin, Pat Hook. Looking on, left to right: Shirley Utting, Unknown, Jean Mummery, Ann Grimble, Pauline Haylock.

The play owed a lot to the work of three teachers, Miss Pennington who trained the singers, Miss Richardson who played the piano accompaniments, and Miss Sheldrick who was responsible for the costumes.

In January 1991 Jack announced his retirement from his job as caretaker of Roman Hill Primary School. Here he is seen as one of the classes say goodbye to him.

The fish market in the early 1960s and the boys gather round for a warm up and a tea-break.

Some of the last Eastern Coachworks apprentices in the early 1980s.

✳   ✳   ✳   ✳   ✳

Ada Roe was one of Lowestoft's oldest residents and was just days off her hundred and twelfth birthday when she died in 1970. Born in Islington she came to Lowestoft with her husband early this century and opened the Victoria Dairy in Clapham Road. He was in ill-health and had been advised that the coastal air might do him some good. Shortly after he arrived though, he died and Ada had to take over the dairy business from him, pushing churns of milk round the streets of the town with a handcart and over the years became quite a local personality.

"If I had one wish," she once said late in her life, "it would be to be young again, say about 80, so I could see my great, great grandchildren grow up....."

A team talk for the TV Manufacturing football team in October 1958 in the newly opened Walmer Road changing rooms. Standing, Charlie Banham (manager), top left: Albert Lacey, Phil Garnham, John Rose, Colin Shears, 'Woof' Batley, 'Lefty' Wright, Terry Crouch. Bottom row: David Bolan, Bruce Parkin, Harry Kinder, Leroy Pitchers.

The Bally Shoe Co. football team in 1980, the last side to be made up completely of the company's employees. The team contained Lowestoft runner Paul Evans, who ran in the 1992 Olympic finals. Back row, left to right: Bob Cheek, Micky Bullard, Dusty Miller, Phil Croft, Pete Pells, Paul Evans, Derrick Leech, Tony Lincoln. Front Row: Warren Bond, Granville Bullock, Danny Tipper, Glen Bocking, Derrick Baker, Garry Reynolds.

In the early 1980s Fred Goldsmith was a regular sight in the town centre, busking with his guitar and mouth organ. Not everyone appreciated him though, and when he bought an electric guitar and amplifier there were comments in the local press and even offers to buy him a songbook! Many took him to their heart though, and when Fred moved on his instantly recognisable 'din' was missed, although the busker does still occasionally visit the town in his travels.

Jack Mitchley, preparing an exhibition in the Bethel, where he was caretaker. Jack was a regular contributor to the Lowestoft Journal in the 'Port Talk' column and had a unique record of all the boats that worked out of Lowestoft. He was also an expert on the town's lifeboat service, writing a booklet on the subject, and he contributed to the early Jack Rose books. He died in 1993 and will be sorely missed.

Some Lowestoft boys watch the motor smack *Pilot Jack* LT1212 leave the harbour in the 1950s. This boat was the last motor smack that Jack Rose shipped on.

Developments

In September 1977 the Clapham Road roundabout was opened although work around it was not completely finished. The motorcycle shop on the left (with the flat roof) has now been exposed to the road and comparing this view with the photograph on the following page, the extent of the demolition work is apparent.

View from St. Peter's Court. The road that runs across the foreground of the picture is St. Peter's Street and all the buildings on the road to the corner (into Clapham Road) were demolished to make way for the new road system. The St. Margaret's Institute can be seen half way down on the extreme left of the photograph.

ROADS

Lowestoft has come a long way since its first road was tarmacked in 1906 when part of the old Yarmouth to London turnpike, a dust bath in the summer and muddy in the winter, was finally given a suitable road surface for its usage. Indeed, since that time much of the town seems to have disappeared under tarmac for new roads one way or another!

The one way system that was completed in the late 1970s has to be the biggest development in the town in the last fifty years. Costing £1.3 million to build, the road was given the go-ahead in November 1972, although the whole scheme had been in the offing for over fifty years! At a lecture in 1922 the then Borough Engineer Mr. S.W. Mobbs advocated many of the 'improvements' which took place in the 1970s. He hoped that they might be in place by 1940 but by that time of course the town had other things on its mind. In 1961 however some of these plans were published in a town centre plan proposing the the creation of a circular one-way system, pedestrianising the town centre and improving traffic flow. The route was confirmed in 1965 but by then a considerable number of properties had been acquired by the Corporation and in the following years the town began to witness large scale demolition work in St. Peter's Street, Duke's Head Street, White Horse Street, Factory Street, The Hemplands, and Crown Street, while there was no trace left of Chapel Street at all! The whole east side of Clapham Road was also reduced to rubble as the roads which were to become Katwijk Way and Jubilee Way began to take shape and were finally completed in 1978.

This was phase one and two of a four phase plan, although phases three and four were not even begun until 1993 when another new road, Artillery Way, was built giving access from the north to the south of the town. Construction of the new road resulted in further demolition of property around the junction of Arnold Street and St. Peter's Street, in addition to changes made to the High Street road layout. A road system that took thirty-three years to complete was always going to be out-dated and during the construction of Artillery Way the authorities took little heed of residents who complained that there was no suitable crossing of a busy road in an area where there are now many flats for the elderly, which of course were not there when the plan was conceived. It also caused a great deal of inconvenience for the High Street's traders, who were cut off from the rest of the town by the new road and a needlessly complicated road layout around them.

Presumably the road took so long to build because of insufficient funding, but with the continual increase of cars on our roads each year, it seems likely that more and more roads will not be an answer. Indeed, the one-way system, responsible for so much destruction and disruption in the town, now seems little more than a temporary measure.

In 1989 another road scheme caused a storm of protest when it was proposed to cut through Normanston Park with a link road to a new £10 million shopping development which was built on the site of the former Eastern Coachworks.

Although a petition against the road was signed by 8,000 people, it was to no avail as in July 1989 the Waveney District Council, who were already committed to the North Quay shopping development, agreed to sell the parkland needed for the road. Construction began in March 1990 and was named Peto Way, ready for the opening of the North Quay Shopping Park in November 1990. It is widely accepted that land adjacent to this retail park is the natural site for the town's third crossing whenever the funding becomes available. Indeed, the final piece in the town's jigsaw of roads will be the A12 spine road, the preferred route of which was announced in 1971. This suggested route will come down from Bloodmoor Road, through vacant land that was once part of a golf course and now adjoins a housing estate, over part of Kirkley Run, through Kirkley Fen joining an intersection at Horn Hill. The next section of the road would cross the harbour and join the North Quay Shopping Park. From Peto Way it seems probable that another road would be built to link up with Pleasurewood Hills and the new Tesco's store situated in Gunton. However, funding for this road won't be available till the beginning of the next century, so don't hold your breath!

A scheme that hopefully won't be introduced was put forward in 1970 when it was announced that part of Belle Vue Park would be taken away so that Yarmouth Road could be turned into a dual carriageway. Such were the protests that the Suffolk County Council admitted they would have to rethink the scheme although they would not completely rule out the possibility of it. However, this did little to abate the storm especially when it was announced that, in any event, the new road wasn't likely to happen until at least 1995!

✳   ✳   ✳   ✳   ✳

Clapham Road was one of the longest residential roads in Lowestoft, running adjacent to London Road North. The new road system overlapped and cut up most of Clapham Road and all the buildings to the right of the photo and all those on the left up to where the tree stands were all demolished.

The site of the car-park was once that of the Co-op which was bombed to the ground by a German air-raid in the last War. When work began on the new road compensation of nearly £100,000 was claimed by Lowestoft Co-operative Society for its site in Clapham Road but only £46,000 was awarded.

On the left can be seen the remainder of Clapham Road, walled off from the new Katwijk Way. In 1975 Clapham Road was, as the Journal stated, ".....full of shattered houses and rubble littered sites...." and looked as if it had been a victim of wartime bombing.

By November 1977, when the picture was taken, the residents on the west side of Clapham Road looked across to a new neighbour - Katwijk Way.

Aerial view of Dowson's Bakery in Chapel Street. In 1967 it stood once again in isolation as all the neighbouring properties were reduced to rubble as part of the road scheme. When Mr. & Mrs Dowson opened up the confectionery shop in 1959 it was surrounded by a tight-knit community of small cottages which were all flattened and are today the site of multi-storey flats, a roundabout and roads. The shop opened for the last time on the 8th September, 1967 and demolition work began soon after and the ancient building, and indeed Chapel Street itself, was no more.

St. Peter's Street in the 1970s before the new road layout cut through the large car park in the bottom left of the photograph. In 1977 a roundabout was built here and the car park was halved, and in 1993 was further reduced when Artillery Way was built.
St. Peter's Church, seen to the right, was also demolished in 1973 but this time not for the road system. It was replaced by Runnymede Court, a block of flats for the elderly.

The new Jubilee Way, seen here during its construction, cutting through many of the oldest streets in the town. The building in the centre of the photo, painted white with a black roof, has the inscription 'LBC' which many think stands for London Brick Company. In fact this stands for Lewis Becket Cooper, an old established Lowestoft business who were in the town from around 1846 before finally closing in May 1963. The council offices are in the one storey building in front of these premises while the next building on the right belonged to Green's the printer and is now the site of Wesley Court, a block of flats.

The new road started in Denmark Road, near the railway station and cut through the houses in Tonning Street and through the site of the *Stone Cottage* public house. Houses on the east side of Raglan Street were knocked down while a new roundabout built north of Till Road also involved a considerable amount of property demolition.

The changes the new road system caused were far-reaching. Suffolk Plain was renamed Station Square and redeveloped with a new road system introduced and is shown here waiting to be landscaped in September 1978. This area was to be the home of the controversial new statue called, 'The Call of the Sea' the work of Aylsham sculptor William Redgrave. The eight foot bronze statue of a fisherman cost £20,000 and was paid for by public subscription but received an indifferent response from locals when it was unveiled in November 1980.

The cost of the London Road North to Gordon Road pedestrianisation was estimated at £166,000 and work began, as shown in the photograph, in the early 1980s. Ironically the bricks that cover the road have to be regularly replaced as they weren't designed to take the weight of the delivery lorries and security vehicles that still have to drive down this 'pedestrianised' area.

Since the war the Corporation had been acquiring property that was in the way of the road scheme. The *Triangle Tavern* in St. Peter's Street was one such property although in the end demolition wasn't necessary. This picture shows the original *Triangle Tavern* in Arnold Street, which can be found at the back of the St. Peter's Street pub. Due to Artillery Way part of this building was taken down brick by brick and oddly enough rebuilt (except without a door) a few feet back. With all the historic buildings that the town has destroyed in the last fifty years it does seem an odd decision to take such care in preserving this particular one!

Looking north at the High Street junction with Old Nelson Street and Artillery Way. Opened in 1993, this road takes traffic behind the High Street and joins up with Jubilee Way. As part of the scheme controversial changes were made to the High Street road layout involving numerous road bumps to reduce the speed of traffic, pebbled areas, and odd parking restrictions which has made life difficult for the High Street traders.

Two photographs of the same view just four years apart. The top photograph was taken in 1990, shortly before work began on the £6.6 million Oulton Broad relief road. To make way for the road, sixteen properties were demolished, while twenty-one frontages were removed from other buildings. The road also involved construction of a new bascule bridge, which was built alongside the old one which had been showing serious signs of wear. The picture below shows the same area today, with the two churches on the right of the photo and Taylor's newsagents (the white building) demolished to accommodate the new road system in addition to other buildings in Victoria Road. The new road has helped relieve traffic in this area, which had been a problem for some time, although it has caused difficulties for traders in Bridge Road and Victoria Road, who have been bypassed, badly signposted and cut off by the new road.

THE BRITTEN CENTRE

In 1985 work began on a new shopping centre which was built on 'The Prairie' off London Road North and took two years to construct, costing £11 million.

The Prairie was the last undeveloped site in the town centre and was part of a four acre site, including the Odeon cinema, that Waveney District Council had long been interested in for redevelopment as a shopping and civic centre. W.H. Smith had bought the shops next to the cinema as early as 1972, so it seems the Odeon's fate had been sealed for quite a while before it was finally demolished in 1979. Another tenant in the Britten Centre complex was B.H.S. who already occupied a store and had a 46,000 square foot extension built to link up with the new Centre.

The Britten Centre was opened on Saturday November 13th, 1987 by 'Doctor Who' actor Peter Davison. Heralded as 'taking Lowestoft shoppers into the 90s', the recession that gripped the country early in this decade has limited its success.

The Prairie, pictured here in the early 1970s, was so-called because it was thought to have been part of a private estate where the deer roamed free in the nineteenth century.

At the time of the photograph, Boots were situated in the shop which can be seen at the top of the Prairie, partly hidden by an old Corporation bus. In the mid-1970s Boots moved down London Road North to new premises built on the site of the Baptist Church, whose spire can be seen in the top right hand corner of the photograph. The large imposing brick building was the rear of the Odeon, one of Lowestoft's most fondly remembered cinemas.

The Odeon's foyer remained largely unchanged during the building's short history and seems to be the most memorable feature of the cinema. It opened in 1937 and was a part of the town for just forty years before its last feature, a James Bond double bill of 'The Spy Who Loved Me' with 'Live and Let Die' was shown on April 25th, 1979. Despite people's fond memories of the Odeon its closure met with apathy and some people who arrived for the last show didn't even know it was closing!

In 1979 the Odeon was demolished to clear the way for the Britten Centre. The cinema had been losing money for some time as simply not enough people were interested in watching films in the late 1970s. Shop-owners had complained too that when the cinema did pull in the crowds, the queues hindered access to their shops. However, probably the chief reason was the cinema's plum site adjoining the undeveloped Prairie area.

By October 1979 the Odeon had gone, revealing a naked-looking Prairie. In the background you can see Lowestoft's new library which had recently been built in 1975. Incidentally, the round white tower on top of the library is actually the boiler room!

The bus station in Gordon Road was also demolished to make way for part of the new shopping centre. The station had quite a history and was originally a theatre built in 1919 at a cost of £10,000. Known as the Regent Alfreso it was most remembered for its ceiling which was painted with the moon and stars like a night sky. In the 1930s the theatre was converted into a bus depot, the actors' changing rooms became the rest room for bus drivers and the open court yard with trees and grass that fronted the building disappeared beneath a concrete forecourt.

In 1987 the area was redeveloped again and the Regent Alfresco bus station was demolished. Part of the site is still used as a bus depot although now the buses themselves are housed down the Whapload Road industrial estate. The part that adjoined the Prairie was turned into a new market place, part of the Britten Centre scheme.

BIRD'S EYE

The first Bird's Eye factory in the town was opened in 1945 and three years later the firm leased a building in Rant Score as a packing station. Development continued and in 1950 a pea-processing line was installed and the packing department extended. Since then the factory has far out-stripped its modest beginnings and is now one of the biggest employers in the town.

This picture shows the Bird's Eye factory in the 1950s, facing north towards Rant Score. Every other building in the photograph has been demolished with much of the area now housing new Bird's Eye factories. On the west side of the road, where the two men are walking, is the Eagle brewery, famous for the two gold eagles that adorned the front of the building. When the brewery was demolished in 1958 although one of the eagles was broken, the other was saved and now sits on the entrance to Bird's Eye's canteen.

See facing pages overleaf.

Aerial view of the Beach Village and surrounding area taken in the mid-1960s. By this time Bird's Eye had begun to take over the area, with their cold store and factories creeping over the Denes. Whapload Road runs from left to right across the centre of the photo, while on the top left the St. Peter's Court flats can be seen under construction.

Also hidden by the Bird's Eye factories is the most easterly point in the country. The few dogged tourists who reach Ness Point each year may be disappointed to find only a small plaque to mark the spot but it is difficult to imagine how Ness Point could be turned into a tourist attraction in an area that is now an industrial estate. It seems that the Town Council have instead turned their attention to the newly named 'East Point' area, situated on the south side of the bridge, which boasts the new glass pavilion. Indeed, the Esplanade is one of the last undeveloped areas in the town and its future has been open to debate for most of this century!

In 1936 a proposal was made to build an outdoor swimming pool and public assembly rooms on part of this land, with a model put on display for the public at the Electric House. Though these plans received something of an indifferent public response, the £135,000 scheme was approved in the late 1930s but was shelved at the outbreak of war and never completed. Those who disagreed with the plan felt that the town needed a covered swimming pool, indeed, the Town Council could have purchased one decades earlier, the Grand Cinema swimming pool, but the deal fell through. Today, although Lowestoft now has an indoor pool within the town's sports centre, many locals feel that the town needs a fun pool and that the Esplanade is still the site where it should be.

Another of the town's newer tourist attractions is Pleasurewood Hills, an American theme park, which was the brainchild of Mr. Joe Larter and was built at Corton and opened in 1983. It seems that when Mr. Larter's children complained of being bored and having nothing to do, he responded as all caring fathers do by providing something. He set up a £2½ million leisure theme park!

Gradually more attractions were added and more people came and in 1989 Joe Larter sold the park to the RKF Group although he remained a shareholder and became Managing Director. This, however, was short-lived as due to the recession RKF went into receivership in January 1991 and for a while the theme park's future hung in the balance. By March though a five man management team, including Mr. Larter, bought the company and Pleasurewood Hills was saved. In recent years the park's reputation has grown and received national acclaim while its mascot, Woody Bear, has become something of a local personality!

✳   ✳   ✳   ✳   ✳

Looking down on to the Denes and the Bird's Eye factories. In 1991 controversy raged over the future use of the Denes following an application by Bird's Eye Walls to extend their factory in Whapload Road. Permission was granted and it now seems we are not far off the day when the rest of the Denes is lost to industry.

East Point Pavilion was built in 1993 at a cost of £1.3 million. The Victorian style glazed building may look old-fashioned but was built from an energy saving design involving solar panels. The building contains three rooms given to the 'Lowestoft Story' where with the aid of modern technology, you can see, hear and smell the town's history!